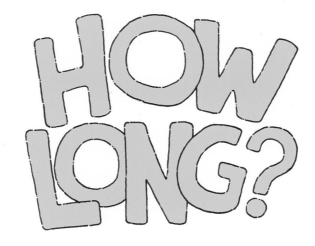

HOW LONG?

TO GO, TO GROW, TO KNOW

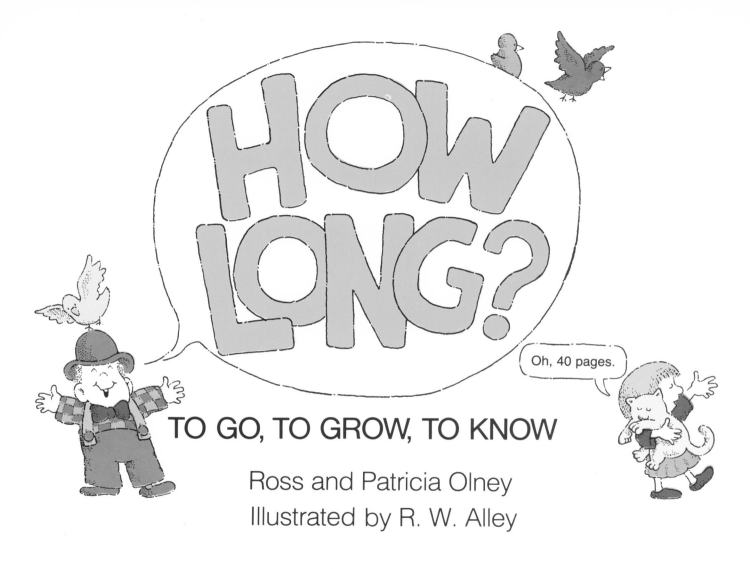

HOW LONG?

Oh, 40 pages.

TO GO, TO GROW, TO KNOW

Ross and Patricia Olney

Illustrated by R. W. Alley

William Morrow and Company   New York   1984

1 2 3 4 5 6 7 8 9 10

Library of Congress Cataloging in Publication Data
Olney, Ross Robert, 1929-   How long?   Summary: Examines in
brief text and illustrations the length of time it takes for various
things to grow, to travel to different places, and to live. Also
discusses the longest river, animal, and word. 1. Time—Juvenile
literature. [1. Time.   2. Measurement] I. Olney, Pat.   II. Alley,
R. W. (Robert W.), ill.   III. Title.
QB209.5.046   1984   529   83-13392
ISBN 0-688-02773-3
ISBN 0-688-02774-1 (lib. bdg.)

HOW
LONG?

CONTENTS

Let's see— some chapters are 6 pages long, some are 7, one is 4, and one's 5.

TO GROW?

All things do not grow at the same speed. Some things grow very fast, while others grow much more slowly. Bermuda grass can grow 6 inches in a day, but one South American fern takes 150 years to become full-grown.

Ocean seaweed, or kelp, can grow as much as 18 inches every day.

One type of bamboo can grow 36 inches in a day, or more than 100 feet in less than 3 months. But as fast as they grow, its stems are still as strong as steel.

Trees usually grow very slowly, but not the *Albizzia falcata*.
It grows more than 35 feet in a year.

The slowest growing tree, a Sitka spruce, grew to only 11 inches
tall in 98 years. It takes up to *3,500 years* for a giant sequoia tree to
become full-size—100 feet around at the bottom and 272 feet tall.

2-year-old whale

100-year-old clam

Can you guess what the fastest and slowest growing animals are? The blue whale is fastest. In less than two years, it grows from an egg weighing only .000035 ounce to its adult weight of more than 29 *tons.* That's nearly 60,000 pounds. Five elephants and you could stand on its back without hurting it.

The slowest growing of all the animals is the deep-sea clam. It takes about 100 years for it to reach a size of less than ½ inch long.

Baby mammals grow inside their mothers before they are born. It took you 9 months to grow inside your mother and the blue whale takes 12 months. But a baby elephant grows inside its mother for nearly 2 years before it is born.

On the other hand, a baby rabbit is born after only 4 weeks, and some baby mice take only 2½ weeks before they are born.

A baby lion or tiger? About 3½ months.

Reptiles can grow very large, but they grow slowly. One python snake grew to 28½ feet long and weighed 320 pounds. That is a *big* snake. It started as a tiny egg and lived nearly 30 years. However, the thread snake is only 4½ inches long fully grown.

What about your own body? Your fingernails grow very slowly.
It takes them about 6 months to grow ½ inch. But your hair grows
½ inch in a month.

My new skin fits fine!

Your skin grows from the inside out. It is always replacing itself, every hour of every day. The top layer keeps rubbing off and every few days you have a new skin. And *your* skin will grow anywhere on *your* body. Doctors often move skin from one part of your body to another if you need it to cover a place that has been injured. The old skin grows in the new spot, and your body grows new skin in the old area. So everything is right again.

Did you know that a piece of your skin as small as a quarter and only $\frac{1}{16}$ to $\frac{1}{8}$ inch thick contains *3 feet* of blood vessels? It also has 4 yards of nerves, 25 nerve ends, 100 sweat glands, and more than *3,000,000* cells. All in that one small area.

Your skin is the largest organ in your body, and a very active one at that.

TO LIVE?

Human beings live for an average of 75 to 80 years.
Some people live much longer than this, to over 100 years.

The Twins, 1904

The Twins—1934

The Twins—1964

The Twins, 1984

But the poor mayfly lives for only a few hours. It doesn't even have a mouth to eat with.

At the other end of the scale of life, scientists say that certain bacteria have remained alive in a deep sleep for over 1,000,000 years. And one type of bacteria actually stayed alive in the same type of deep sleep for over *600,000,000 years*. Then it returned to wide-awake life.

Cats have been known to live 35 years and dogs up to about 30 years, though most live from 10 to 15 years. Turtles, perhaps because they are so slow moving, often live to well over 100 years.

If you didn't run around so much, you'd live longer.

But if we moved as slowly as you, we would never get anywhere.

Trees live longer than any other living thing, not counting bacteria.

One bristlecone pine in California is still alive after *4,600 years*. It is named "Methuselah." Scientists say that if it is left alone, it can live another 1,000 years.

But for a tree, that isn't living so long. Many giant sequoias live to be more than 6,000 years old.

I'm 4,600 years old.

That's nothing, sonny— I'm 6,000 years old.

14

And if you think that is a long time, consider one species of Japanese cedar. Some trees of this species have been proven to be over *7,000 years* old and are still living. That is *old*.

TO GO?

Do you know how long it would take to get to the nearest star? If you had to *walk* there?

It would take more than 1,000,000,000 years to walk to *Proxima Centauri*, the closest star to Earth. That's one *billion* years.

Nobody could do that, of course.

GALACTIC INFO

Proxima Centauri? Only another 750,000 years to go!

It would be much quicker to walk to the moon. That would take only about 13 years, if you didn't stop to eat or sleep.

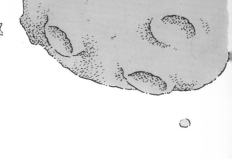

Astronauts can get to the moon in only 2 days. They fly there in very fast spaceships.

You might be able to do that too, if you want to. Someday.

One man walked across the United States in 53½ days.
You could do that today.

But it would be faster to fly across in a jet plane.
That would take you only 5 hours. A train makes
it across the United States in about 3 days and
a car in about 5 days, with some time out for
the driver to rest.

PACIFIC
OCEAN

ATLANTIC
OCEAN

The same trip took pioneers several
months in wagon trains, if they were lucky.

You could walk around the famous Indianapolis Motor Speedway in about an hour if no race cars were there. The Speedway is 2½ miles around. This is about 40 to 50 blocks in your town. You could ride the distance on a bicycle in perhaps 15 minutes.

It takes A.J. Foyt only 45 seconds in his race car. That's covering a *lot* of distance in less than one minute.

He seems to be going as fast as lightning. But he isn't. If he were racing with a lightning bolt or a beam of light, old A.J. would

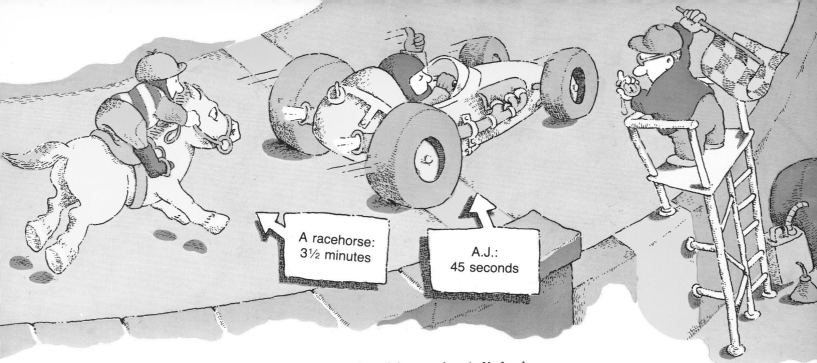

A racehorse:
3½ minutes

A.J.:
45 seconds

be left far behind no matter how fast his car is. A light beam or bolt of lightning would cover that same 2½ miles distance in only .000013 second. That's *really* fast.

A racehorse could run around the Speedway in about 3½ minutes.

But an ant, hurrying as fast as possible, would cross the finish line 37 hours after it started. And a snail would glide around in 13¾ days. Forty or fifty blocks is a great distance to a snail or an ant.

Speaking of going, can you guess how far a frog can jump? One frog in the Calaveras County Jumping Frog Jubilee jumped over 17 feet in one great leap. And that isn't even a *really* big leap.

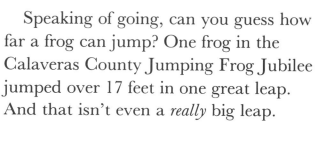

A flea once jumped a full 13 inches, reaching a height of over 7 inches. That was a jump of more than 130 times its own height. It would be the same as you jumping straight up as high as two football fields stacked end to end.

TO LAST?

Like your top layer of skin, which rubs off every few days, your body won't last forever. But it could last much longer. Scientists say that if we could keep our bodies cooler, at around 86 degrees, we would live at least 200 years.

Unfortunately, we can't. Not only is our body temperature automatic, but we couldn't stay that cool and still enjoy a normal life.

Your body is like a machine, with many parts working together. If it were a *real* machine, spare parts could be installed when something wore out. Then your body would last much longer. Today some parts can be replaced, and there will be more replaceable parts in the future.

An automobile can last almost forever because all of its parts are replaceable. Some cars are still being driven after *1,000,000 miles*.

Those car owners take *very* good care of their cars, of course.

24

A television set would last much longer if you just left it on all the time. It is the turning off and on that wears it out the most. But the extra electricity you would use to keep the set on all the time would make the whole idea cost too much.

You can tell how long a light bulb will last by reading its package. It will usually burn for 1,000 hours or more, but not much longer. Some bulbs, called long-life bulbs, will last longer. But they cost more, too. Early-day bulbs often burned for only a few hours.

EXIT

Runs great!

OLD PARTS BIN

NEW PARTS

NEW PARTS

NEW PARTS

25

Can you guess how long the four great stone-faces at Mount Rushmore will last? At least 100,000 years. They were carved from hard granite. By the time they begin to wear out, people may have forgotten who Jefferson, Washington, Lincoln, and Roosevelt were.

On a hot day, a drop of rain might last only a few seconds before it evaporates back into the air. But the same drop might last until spring if it falls as a snowflake in the middle of winter.

If the drop of water fell on a rock, it would appear to just splash. But really it is wearing away a very tiny bit of the rock. Still, it would take hundreds of years for raindrops to wear away a rock the size of a basketball.

Unless the water got *inside*, into a crack in the rock. Then in only one winter the raindrops could freeze and expand, breaking the rock into pieces.

If a worker hit the same rock with a sledge hammer, it would break apart with only a few blows. The rock would break even quicker if the worker used a jackhammer to bang on it. Of course, a big steamroller would reduce the rock to powder with only one heavy pass.

TO KNOW?

It seems as if you know instantly the things that your eyes and ears tell you. That is not true. You see the words on this page *almost* instantly. But not quite. It takes light a brief split second to get from the page to your eyes.

The same is true when you look at the sun (through very dark glass, of course, or your eyes can be injured). It takes about 8 minutes for the light to travel to your eyes from the sun.

It takes *hundreds of years* for the light from some stars to reach Earth. So what you are seeing when you look at the sky on a cloudless night actually happened hundreds of years ago.

Radar devices use radio waves. These waves move through air as fast as light, 186,000 miles per second.

Sonar devices, which are used to detect objects underwater, use sound waves. And sound travels much slower than light does. In the water a sound wave travels about 4,800 feet per second, and 1,100 feet a second in the air.

You can see this difference between the speed of light waves and sound waves for yourself. During a storm, you usually see the lightning before you hear the sound of thunder, even though they both happen at the same time. The light from the lightning got to you much quicker than the sound from the thunder.

You can even measure how far away the lightning is. For every five seconds of difference between the flash of light and the sound, the lightning struck a mile away. Seven seconds would be about a mile and a half away. Two or three seconds would be about a half-mile away.

You can also *feel* the vibrations of the sound waves.

This is noticeable where there are very loud noises. If you stand near a drag racer's powerful, loud engine, the skin on your face bounces and ripples from the waves.

Sound moves as fast as light when it travels over a telephone wire or down from a satellite. This is because the sound waves have been changed into radio waves. The sound gets from the satellite to your TV set *much* quicker than it gets from your TV set to your ears across the room. In the last few feet it has become regular sound waves again, and they go much slower.

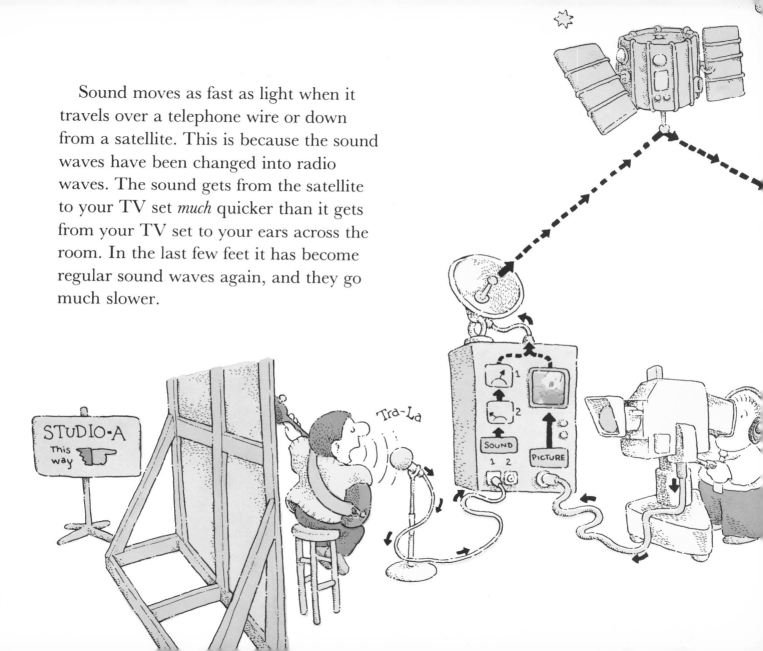

Most people can hear sound waves up to about 20,000 cycles per second. A cycle is one wave, so people can hear up to about 20,000 waves per second. This would be a very high squeal.

Bats, on the other hand, can detect sound waves up to about 150,000 cycles per second. This is much too high for the human ear to hear.

IS?

Remember the jumping flea? It was about $\frac{1}{16}$ inch long, which is the average length for a flea. This is pretty small, but millions of germs can live very comfortably on a flea's back. And thousands of fleas can live on the back of an average dog. Hundreds of dogs could play on the back of a blue whale and never bother the whale at all.

one germ

one flea
with millions
of germs

one dog
with thousands of fleas
with millions of germs

So how many germs are on the blue whale? There isn't enough space in this book to write such a large number.

one blue whale
with hundreds of dogs
with thousands of fleas
with millions of germs

The longest animal ever known is a ribbon worm. This animal swims in the North Sea and one was found to be 180 feet long.

The smallest bird of all is the bee hummingbird. It is only 2.2 inches long fully grown and that includes the beak and the tail. This tiny bird weighs less than ½ ounce. And it stays very close to home.

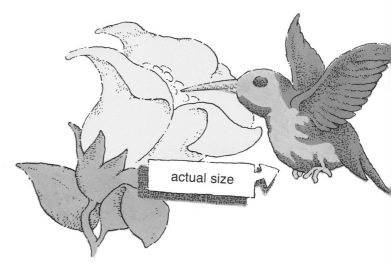

actual size

But the Arctic tern has been known to fly more than 12,000 miles from home. That is a long distance to fly.

The tern could easily fly from one end to the other of the world's longest river. This is the Nile River in Africa. It is 4,187 miles long.

The next longest is the Amazon River in South America. The Amazon is 4,000 miles long.

The Mississippi River in the United States is 13th in line in the world. Yet it is still very long. It is 2,348 miles long and goes from the top of the country to the bottom.

This book is full of words. One of the shortest words has been used here several times. The word is "a." "I" is another short word.

The *longest* word is used on this page, although it is almost never used because it is so long and complicated.

It did appear in a comedy by a Greek writer named Aristophanes, though, back in 400 B.C. There are *182 letters* in it. It starts out "lopadotemachoselacho . . ." and ends up with "traganopterygon."

What does it mean? It is the name of a drink made up of many different things.

LOPADOTEMACHOSELACHO-
GALEOKRANIOLEIPSANODRIM-
HYPOTRIMMATOSILPHIOPARA-
OMELITOKATAKECHYME-
NOKICHLEPIKOSSYPHOPHAT-
TOPERISTERALEKTRYONOP-
TEKEPHALLIOKIGKLOPELE-
IOLAGOIOSIRAIOBAPHE-
TRAGANOPTERYGON

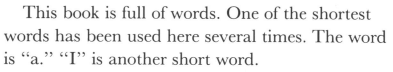

ATHENS

There are other rarely used long words, but one long word is often used by doctors. It is 39 letters long and describes a certain gall bladder operation. Here it is, in case you ever want to use it:

"hepaticocholangiocholecystenterostomies."

One last "how long" just for fun. The longest palindromic word (a word that is spelled the same forward and backward) in the English language is "redivider." That isn't so long, but then there aren't very many such words, either.

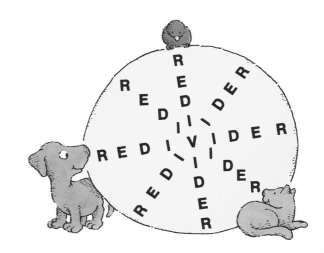

Now, how long did it take you to read this book?